921   Epstein, Samuel,
FER   1909—.

c.1

        Enrico Fermi,
          father of atomic
          power

DATE			

Americans All biographies are inspiring life stories about people of all races, creeds, and nationalities who have uniquely contributed to the American way of life. Highlights from each person's story develop his contributions in his special field — whether they be in the arts, industry, human rights, education, science and medicine, or sports.

Specific abilities, character, and accomplishments are emphasized. Often despite great odds, these famous people have attained success in their fields through the good use of ability, determination, and hard work. These fast-moving stories of real people will show the way to better understanding of the ingredients necessary for personal success.

Enrico Fermi

FATHER OF ATOMIC POWER

by Sam and Beryl Epstein

illustrated by Raymond Burns

GARRARD PUBLISHING COMPANY
CHAMPAIGN, ILLINOIS

A Note to the Reader

Enrico Fermi liked to talk with school children and explain things to them. He used to say that the future of our country rests on the younger generations. I am very glad that Sam and Beryl Epstein have written this lively story of his life, and that through it Fermi can go on talking to young people. I believe that you will enjoy reading this book.

Laura Fermi

Laura Fermi

Picture credits:

Fermi, Laura, *Atoms in the Family: My Life with Enrico Fermi* (Chicago: University of Chicago, 1954): p. 10, 18, 44 (both), 57, 70, 90, 92

Bettmann Archive: p. 73

Brown Brothers: p. 2, 86

Wide World: p. 79, 94

Contents

1. Brothers

"What shall we do this afternoon? Shall we try to make that electric motor we talked about? Or shall we draw another plan for an airplane?"

Enrico Fermi, eleven years old, was talking to his twelve-year-old brother, Giulio. It was a gray, wintry day in 1912. The Fermi brothers were walking home from school together, as they always did. They lived in the great city of Rome, in Italy.

Enrico and Giulio knew that thousands of people came to Rome every year. These visitors came from all over the world to see the city's many famous sights. They visited Rome's Colosseum, built by a Roman emperor almost two thousand years earlier, and the great church of St. Peter's, where, it was said, St. Peter himself was buried.

Enrico and Giulio were not much interested in the ancient buildings of Rome. They thought airplanes, which were still very new in 1912, were much more exciting.

Giulio said, "I heard today that somebody invented a seaplane—a plane that can land on water. Maybe we should try to make a plan for that kind of airplane."

"That's a wonderful idea!" Enrico said. Then he added, "But when are we going to make the motor?"

There were always too many things to do, Enrico thought. He and Giulio never had time enough for all of them.

Giulio began to walk faster. He was tall for his age. Enrico was much smaller and had short legs, but somehow he managed to keep up. He never wanted anyone to get ahead of him, not even his big brother.

Soon they reached the apartment house where they lived.

"We are going to make a plan for a seaplane!" Enrico told their mother.

"Finish your homework first," she said.

Enrico and Giulio sighed. Their mother was a schoolteacher. She wanted to make sure the boys had a good education. So did their father. He himself had had only a few years of schooling. His poor education had made it necessary for him to work hard for a long time in order to win his good job in the office of the Italian railroads.

The boys shivered as they took out their schoolbooks. Very few apartments in Rome were heated at that time, and their study room was cold.

Giulio and Enrico Fermi

Enrico propped his history book up on the table, so that he did not have to hold it. Then he sat down and tucked his icy hands under his legs, to warm them. Giulio did the same thing. .

Soon their sister Maria, a year older than Giulio, brought her schoolbooks to the table too. She kept her hands warm inside the sleeves of her dress.

When Enrico came to the end of a page, he didn't want to bring his hands out into the cold air. He had an idea.

"Look!" he said to Giulio. "I'm going to turn the page without using my hands."

He bent close to the book. He stuck out his tongue. With the tip of his tongue, he flicked up the corner of the page and turned it over.

"Enrico!" Maria said. "That is disgusting!"

Giulio laughed. "You are a genius!" he told Enrico.

Enrico grinned at him. He had known Giulio would think it was funny, and clever too. He and Giulio always understood each other.

The two brothers were almost always together. But one day a few years later

Enrico had to set off for school alone. Giulio had a sore throat and his mother was keeping him at home in bed. Enrico felt strange and lonely going to school by himself. He hoped Giulio would be well by the next day.

The next day Giulio was worse. He was no better the day after that.

"There is an abscess in his throat," the doctor said. "We will have to remove it."

Giulio tried to grin at Enrico as he was taken to the hospital. "We'll do that experiment with electricity as soon as I come home," he whispered.

Giulio never returned from the hospital. He died even before the operation could be performed. Enrico's mother and his sister Maria cried for many days. Enrico did not cry at all. He knew that tears could not bring back the brother who had been his best friend.

2. "A Very Exceptional Young Man"

Enrico Fermi was thirteen years old when his brother died. For many long months afterward, he felt alone in the world. His only friends were the kind of books he and Giulio had once read and studied together. They were books about mathematics and science.

His father had few books on those subjects. The Italian schools of that time had even fewer. The only way Enrico could get new books was to buy them, and he did not have much money to spend. So Wednesday afternoons he went to the big open-air market that was held in Rome each week.

There people bought and sold all kinds of things — vegetables, cheeses, spaghetti, old clothes, used furniture, and second-hand books.

One Wednesday Enrico found a book about physics at his favorite second-hand book stall. Physics was one subject that interested him very much. It is the science of energy — of motion, heat, light, sound and electricity — and deals with the behavior of elements. To a scientist an element is any substance made up of atoms, or tiny particles, that are all alike. Gold is an element because all its atoms are exactly alike. Water is not an element because it is made up of two kinds of atoms — atoms of the element hydrogen and atoms of the element oxygen.

As Enrico was glancing through the book, a voice beside him said, "Aren't you the brother of Giulio Fermi?"

Enrico looked up from the book. The boy who had spoken to him was a little older than he was. Enrico nodded silently.

"I was sure I had seen you with him," the boy said. "I knew Giulio at school. My name is Enrico Persico."

Enrico didn't want to talk about Giulio. All he said was, "My name is Enrico too."

"Then we are lucky!" Enrico Persico said. "We shall never forget each other's names. Are you buying that book on physics?" he asked.

"I think so," Enrico answered. "I am very interested in physics. But I am interested in mathematics too. It is my best subject in school. Perhaps I'll spend my money on a mathematics book."

"I have some books about mathematics that I could lend you," Enrico Persico said. "And you could lend me this book if you

16

buy it. Or maybe we could read and study our books together."

From that moment on the two Enricos were friends. They exchanged books. They did experiments together. Together they tried to find answers to the questions they were always asking.

Soon Enrico made another new friend, an engineer who worked with his father. When Enrico learned that this man was a college graduate, he asked him many questions about mathematics and science.

The engineer answered Enrico's questions with great patience. He was interested in helping a young boy who was so eager to learn. Then he said, "I will lend you one of my own books on mathematics. It is very difficult. There are many problems in it that I cannot even solve myself, but perhaps you will be able to understand a little of it."

17

Enrico raced through the book and returned it to the engineer.

"Were you able to solve any of the problems?" the man asked.

"I solved them all," Enrico said.

The engineer was amazed. "I want to help your son all I can," he told Enrico's father. "He's a born mathematician. I will lend him all my books."

When Enrico finished high school, mathematics was still one of his favorite subjects.

At sixteen, Enrico was interested in science as well as mathematics

"Do you think you'll be a mathematician?" Enrico Persico asked him.

Enrico had been asking himself that same question. "No," he said after a moment of thought. "I have decided that I want to be a physicist."

He had come to feel that mathematics alone would not satisfy him. He wanted to use his mathematics as a tool to help him explore some of the mysteries of science.

When he told his parents about his plan, they were pleased. They said he could go on living at home and study at the University of Rome.

The engineer disagreed. He told the Fermis that Enrico should go to a college in the city of Pisa. "Pisa has been a center of learning for hundreds of years," he said. "Students come to Italy from all over Europe to study there. It is a place where new ideas are always in the air. It is just the kind of place Enrico needs. And I'm sure," he added, "that Enrico will be able to win a scholarship there."

He was right. Although Enrico was younger than many of the students who took the examination for the scholarship, he got higher marks than all of them.

After the examination a professor at the Pisa college called Enrico to his office.

"How old are you?" the professor asked the small, dark young man.

"Seventeen," Enrico told him.

The professor shook his head. "Then I do not understand how you were able to answer some of those questions in physics as well as you did," he said. "I did not think a seventeen-year-old boy could know so much. You are a very exceptional young man! Yes, very exceptional indeed!"

3. Theory, Tricks and a Stink Bomb

The small city of Pisa is near the coast north of Rome. Enrico lived there in a room in the ancient stone palace that housed his school.

"It is freezing cold here in winter," one of the older students told him. "There is no heat in the building."

Enrico laughed. "I'm used to that," he said. He showed the student the small clay jug he had found in his room. "What is this for?" he asked.

"You put hot coals in it," the student explained. "Then, when your hands get icy cold, you warm them by holding the jug."

Enrico laughed again. "I'm certainly not used to that!" he said. "A warm jug for my hands will be a luxury."

One of the first places Enrico wanted to see was the tall, round building called the Leaning Tower of Pisa. This famous tower leaned so far over that it seemed about to fall.

Enrico climbed to the top of the tower. "Now," he said to himself, "I am standing where Galileo stood more than 300 years ago!"

The great Italian scientist Galileo was one of Enrico's heroes. Enrico knew the story about him that all young Italians were told. According to this story Galileo wanted to prove that heavy things do not

22

fall faster than light things, as people in his time believed. So he carried a large stone and a small stone to the top of the tower and dropped them at the same time. They both struck the ground at the same instant. He had proved that light and heavy things fall at the same speed.

Enrico said to himself, "I could make the same experiment Galileo made from the very same place!" Then he thought, "But the stones might hit somebody!"

Another one of Enrico's heroes was still living. He was the famous German-born physicist Albert Einstein, and he too had theories that seemed strange to the world of his day. They had to do with light and energy, and the movement of the stars and planets. Einstein built up his theories by making long and complicated mathematical calculations.

Enrico studied those calculations until he understood them. Then he could understand Einstein's theories, which even some of Enrico's professors could not understand. One of the professors asked Enrico to explain Einstein's ideas to him. Enrico did.

Enrico found that Pisa was as exciting a place as the engineer had said it would be. He liked the laboratory experiments he carried out. He liked reading about the many new theories that scientists were then working out. Some of the most interesting ones, he thought, had to do with the atom. Atoms fascinated Fermi because there were so many questions about them that scientists could not yet answer.

Physicists did know that the tiny atom was made up of even smaller particles. At its center was a core, or nucleus. Tiny particles called electrons spun around the nucleus, like planets spinning around the sun. Physicists also knew that some atoms sent out rays, which were really particles of the atoms shooting out into space. Atoms that behaved in this way, such as the atoms of the element radium, were called radioactive.

Still, many things about the atom were unknown. Enrico began to dream that some day he might become the kind of physicist who could work out new theories about such mysteries. To do that, he realized, he would have to know a great deal. He studied hard.

He was not spending all his time studying physics, however. His best friend at college, a physics student named Franco Rasetti, was an expert in certain fields about which Fermi knew almost nothing. So Fermi had to take the time to learn the things Rasetti knew. Fermi still did not like anyone to be ahead of him in any way.

Rasetti was an expert on plants and insects, for example. Fermi listened to him talk about them. He looked at the plants and insects Rasetti showed him when they walked together in the countryside near Pisa. Soon Fermi too was talking like an expert on plants and insects.

Rasetti was also an expert at playing tricks on his friends. He showed Fermi how to balance a pail of water above the door of a student's room. When the student opened the door, the pail tipped over and poured water over him. Soon Fermi was an expert at that, too.

Then Fermi began to invent his own tricks. Once he led a crowd of students to the house where Rasetti lived. Rasetti was still asleep. Fermi put a big padlock on the outside of the door, so that it could not be opened from the inside.

When Rasetti woke up, he could not get out of his room. He ran to a window and shouted angrily down into the street. Fermi led the chorus of cheers and laughter that answered him.

"That's one trick you never even thought of!" Fermi called up to his friend.

One day Fermi and Rasetti made a stink bomb in their chemistry laboratory. They set it off in the classroom. They thought it was a great joke.

Their chemistry professor did not laugh. "You will pay for this," he told them. "I will have you both thrown out of the college!"

Fermi and Rasetti were frightened.

"We won't get our degrees!" Rasetti said.

"We will never be able to work as physicists!" Fermi said.

He knew that a physicist could probably not find a job anywhere then except in a university. In Italy, at that time, few industries hired physicists. He also knew that no university would hire a man who had not won his degree.

Their physics professor came to their rescue. "Fermi and Rasetti are brilliant students," he told everyone. "If they are forced to leave school, Italy will lose two good scientists."

At last the two young men were forgiven. They were permitted to remain in school. Fermi was graduated in July, 1922. Then he discovered that even with his degree he could not do the kind of work he most wanted to do.

4. Congratulations!

In 1922, when Enrico Fermi left Pisa, his country was going through a kind of revolution.

Ever since the end of World War I, in 1918, Italy had been growing poorer. Many Italians were out of work. They were angry at the king and his government, believing that they did nothing for the poor people. More and more the Italian people began to listen to a man who said he could make Italy rich and strong again. His name was Benito Mussolini.

Thousands of people believed Mussolini. They joined the new political party he started, called the Fascist party. The party grew more and more powerful. Finally it demanded that the king make Mussolini his prime minister, the head of his government. The king gave in, and Benito Mussolini became prime minister of Italy at just about the time Fermi returned to Rome.

Fermi understood what had happened. He knew that Mussolini had actually become the dictator of Italy. But Fermi believed such things should not concern him.

"I am a scientist," he said. "I have nothing to do with politics. I must look for a job."

He asked advice from an important man, Professor Orso Mario Corbino, who was a statesman, a businessman, and director of the department of physics at the University of Rome.

"I can see that you understand the important new ideas in the field of physics,"

Professor Corbino said after he had talked with Fermi. "My physics department needs young men like you to teach our students up-to-date physics," he went on. "Unfortunately, I cannot hire you right now. At present things are too unsettled in the government for me to make changes here."

"I understand," Fermi said.

"But you must keep on with your work," the professor said. "I will arrange for you to study with some of the fine German physicists."

Professor Corbino kept his word. Fermi spent seven months in Germany. When he returned to Rome, Professor Corbino still could not hire him for his physics department, but Fermi did get a job at the university, teaching mathematics.

His old friend Enrico Persico said, "I would be glad to have your job, Enrico.

But you must feel sorry because you are not teaching physics."

"No I don't," Fermi told him. "Feeling sorry for myself would be a waste of time. I am very practical, Enrico. I'd feel sorry for myself if it would do me any good. But it wouldn't, so I don't."

"But what about those physics problems you are always trying to solve?" Enrico Persico asked. "Do you have any spare time to spend on them?"

"Oh, yes," Fermi said. "And I can read the books in the university library, and read the reports of what other physicists are doing. Don't worry! Inside my head I am still a physicist!

"Are you coming out to the country with us this weekend?" he asked. "We're going on our bicycles and taking our lunch. In the afternoon we'll play soccer."

Enrico Persico grinned. He was thinking about how much Enrico Fermi had changed from the quiet boy he had first met. Now Fermi was the leader of a lively group of students and young teachers. They all went to the country together almost every weekend. Fermi always planned the trips and told everyone what to do.

Sometimes one of the young men or women said, "Fermi is too bossy!" Another would

36

always answer, "But we always have fun when we do what he suggests."

One day Fermi received an important letter. It came from the University of Leyden, in The Netherlands. It invited Fermi to visit that university and study with a well-known Dutch physicist.

"It was a wonderful three months!" Fermi told Enrico Persico when he returned. "I made some good friends. I learned a lot.

Maybe my new friends learned something from me too."

He also had some good news to tell Enrico Persico. "You are going to take over my teaching job here in Rome," he said. "I have a new job at the University of Florence. I'll teach mathematics there, but I will also teach physics!"

Fermi enjoyed living and working in the beautiful old city of Florence. "My friend, Franco Rasetti from the college in Pisa, is here too!" he reported to his old friends in Rome. "He is still up to his old tricks. On Sundays we go to the country and collect little live lizards. On Mondays we let them loose in the place where the students eat. You should hear the girls scream!"

One day Fermi was lying on a hillside outside of Florence. He and Rasetti had been hunting lizards.

"I've got it!" Fermi cried suddenly.

"Another lizard?" Rasetti asked.

"No! The theory I have been trying to work out for months!" Fermi said. "I think I know now why those atom particles behave as they do in what we call a perfect gas!"

Many people would not have understood what Fermi was talking about. Rasetti did.

"Congratulations!" he said. "Write it down. Publish it. I think it is really important."

Fermi described his theory in a report that was printed in two scientific magazines, one Italian, one German. Many scientists read the report. They said that Fermi had made an important contribution to the science of theoretical physics. He was 24 years old.

5. Professor Fermi's Extravagance

Not long after Fermi formulated his theory on atom particles, he received a letter from Professor Corbino at the University of Rome. The professor said he was finally able to create a position for a professor of theoretical physics at the university. He wanted Fermi to fill it, but he could not simply appoint him to the post. The job had to be given to the physicist who earned the highest marks on a special examination. "Will you compete?" the professor asked.

Fermi was the youngest man to take the difficult examination. He got the highest mark and won the competition.

"Full professor at your age!" Rasetti said when Fermi told him the news. "I never heard of such a thing." He grinned. "There must be some older men who think they should have won the job. You may get into trouble with them."

"Then you can help me get out of it," Fermi answered. He was grinning too. "You are going to be my chief assistant."

The two young physicists hurried to Rome. Together they planned the courses they would teach.

"We are going to do a lot of work on our own," Fermi told Professor Corbino. "We shall try to learn more about how atoms behave, for one thing. We plan to let our students work right along with us," he added. "It will be valuable experience for them."

"Good!" Professor Corbino said. "But don't be too hopeful of your students. Most clever young students study engineering these days. They know engineers can get good jobs in industry."

"But physics is so much more exciting!" Fermi said. "There is so much to learn and discover in this field."

Professor Corbino smiled. "I agree," he said. "I will tell some of our clever engineering students that."

Soon two engineering students left their own department to study with Fermi and Rasetti. The young teachers took their students to parties and on weekend trips into the country. They sat up late talking to them about the mysteries of the atom and how they could try to solve those mysteries.

The four young men—the two teachers and the two students—worked together as a team. They wrote reports that were read by scientists all over the world. Some of these scientists came to Rome to talk to Fermi about his ideas or to study with him. The physics department at the University of Rome was becoming famous.

One day Fermi told his friends, "I have been very careful of my money for a long time. Now I think I can afford to do something foolish, something extravagant."

"What are you going to do?" they all wanted to know.

"I have not made up my mind yet," Fermi said. "But I intend to do one of two things. Either I shall buy a car, or I shall get married."

His friends looked quickly at pretty dark-haired Laura Capon, a student at the university. She often joined them at their parties and on their trips into the country. Everyone had noticed that Fermi was spending more and more time with Laura.

Enrico, above, enjoys an outing in the country and, below, shows off his new car to Laura.

But a few days later Fermi bought a little yellow car. If Laura was disappointed, he didn't seem to notice. He took his friends everywhere in his car. Laura was usually on the front seat beside him.

In a few months Fermi decided that he could afford both a car and a wife. He and Laura were married.

Laura planned a study for Fermi in their new apartment. She bought a big table with plenty of room on it for his papers. She bought a bookcase and a few chairs. The room had no other furniture.

"This is just what I want!" Fermi said.

He was an early riser. By half-past five almost every morning, he was in his study. There he stayed for two hours of intense work. He read. He thought. He made the calculations that he hoped would lead him to a new theory about atoms.

Laura sometimes sat with him and helped him when she could. She was proud of her young husband. She was especially proud when he was chosen as a member of Italy's new Royal Academy. The dictator Mussolini had formed the Academy as part of his plan to show the entire world that Italy was a great country. Its 30 members were chosen from among the most brilliant men in Italy.

Fermi was glad to have the salary every Academy member received, but he didn't like the uniforms the Academy members sometimes had to wear. The jacket and trousers were decorated with silver. The uniform also included a big cape and a sword.

"And this hat is the worst of all!" he told Laura. "It is ridiculous! It has feathers on it!"

The next year Fermi received a different kind of honor. He was invited to lecture

at the University of Michigan in the United States. Fermi was delighted.

"I shall teach myself English before we go," he told Laura. "You are lucky. You have studied the language."

Laura was worried. "But suppose people do not understand my English?" she said.

"Nonsense!" Fermi said.

But when they reached the United States Laura said, "I was right! Today I went out shopping for the first time, and the shopkeeper could not understand what I wanted."

Fermi sighed. "Nobody could understand my lecture either," he said. "But two Dutch professors have promised to listen to my lectures and write down the words I do not say correctly. After each lecture they will give me an English lesson." By the end of the summer Fermi's students could understand him.

During the next few years other American universities invited Fermi to lecture in the United States. Fermi was always happy to accept the invitations. Laura could not go with him on those short visits. By this time she was needed at home to look after their two children, Nella and Giulio.

Sometimes, when Fermi returned from the United States, he said, "Perhaps we should go there to live."

"How can you suggest such a thing?" Laura always said. "We are Italians. Italy is our home."

"Of course," Fermi agreed. "But Italy is changing. We may not want to live here always under the rule of Mussolini."

But his work kept him busy. And as in the past, when he was occupied, he did not worry about the dictator. In 1934 Fermi's work took a new turn.

6. Atomic Experiments

"We are going to experiment with atoms," Fermi told the members of his team in 1934. "I am going to be an experimental physicist for a while. I made up my mind about this as soon as I read the new report from France."

The members of his team had read the same report. It told about an experiment performed by two French physicists, Irène and Frédéric Joliot. Irène Joliot was the daughter of the famous Marie Curie, discoverer of radium.

The Joliots had placed the element aluminum near a radioactive substance that was shooting off tiny particles of atoms called alpha particles. When these particles struck, or bombarded, the aluminum, the nuclei of some of the aluminum atoms changed. For a short time those aluminum atoms also "shot off" particles. They had been made radioactive.

"The Joliots have done an amazing thing," Fermi said. "Man has never before changed an ordinary substance into a radioactive one! Now we shall bombard other elements with atomic particles and see what happens."

"What elements shall we use in our experiments?" a student asked.

"All of them, if we can," Fermi said. "We shall start with the lightest one, hydrogen.

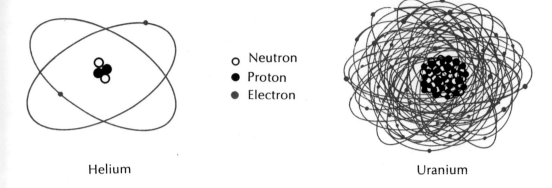

Helium

Uranium

Fermi experimented with light elements like helium, with only 2 electrons, and heavy elements like uranium, with 92 electrons.

Then we shall work our way straight through to the heaviest element, uranium."

"And will we bombard them with alpha particles, as the Joliots did?" asked another student.

"No," Fermi said. "We shall use neutrons. I know it will not be easy, but I have an idea they will make better atomic bullets."

Neutrons, which had been discovered less than two years earlier, are tiny particles inside the central core, or nucleus, of an atom.

52

They do not shoot out of radioactive atoms by themselves, as alpha particles do. To get neutrons for his experiments, therefore, Fermi first had to make a neutron "gun." It was a small glass tube which contained some radioactive material and a small quantity of the element beryllium. When flying alpha particles from the radioactive material hit the beryllium nucleus, some of the beryllium's neutrons were knocked loose and sent shooting out like bullets.

Before Fermi and his team could start their experiments they also had to have a Geiger counter, an instrument that measures

Geiger Counter

radioactivity. Without it they would not know whether or not they had changed an element into a radioactive substance.

The Geiger counter had been invented only a short time earlier. No company manufactured counters for sale. Fermi and his team had to make their own. As soon as the counter was finished, the scientists began their experiments.

At first they were disappointed. They bombarded several elements with neutrons. None of the elements became radioactive.

Then their luck changed. One element became radioactive. Then another and another. It seemed as if many of the heavier elements could be changed by neutron bombardment.

"Come home immediately!" Fermi wrote to Rasetti, who was on a vacation at the time. "Exciting things are going on here!"

Within a few months Fermi and his team had changed about 40 elements into radioactive substances. Sometimes the radioactivity lasted only a few seconds. Sometimes it lasted longer.

They wrote reports of their work. Scientists in many lands read those reports with great interest.

Finally Fermi began to experiment with the heaviest element known, uranium. The bombardment created a new radioactivity in the element. But something else happened too. Some of the uranium atoms changed into substances that Fermi did not recognize. He could not find out what they were by testing them, because these substances appeared in such tiny quantities.

"What can they be?" he wondered.

"Perhaps you have created a new element, sir," one student suggested.

"What nonsense!" another one said, and laughed.

Scientists at that time believed that all elements had been in existence since the beginning of the earth. Some were easy to find—hydrogen, oxygen and iron, for example. Scientists had known about them for a long time. Others, like radium, were very scarce and hard to find. That was why it had taken scientists so long to discover them. Marie Curie had not discovered radium until 1898.

No one had ever believed that man himself could create an element that did not already exist somewhere in nature. Fermi, however, thought it was possible that he had done so.

His report of the experiment said that when he bombarded uranium with neutrons, some of the uranium atoms turned into unknown substances. He wrote that some

The simple laboratory in Rome where Fermi and his team experimented with uranium.

of those substances might someday prove to be new elements. He also wrote that scientists would need to do a great deal of work before they would know for certain whether it was actually possible to produce new elements by bombarding uranium with neutrons.

Years would go by before scientists agreed that Fermi had probably created a few atoms of a new element in his Rome laboratory that day. By then others had made the element, too. It was named neptunium.

As soon as Mussolini's newspapermen heard about Fermi's report, however, they spread the story far and wide. They did not use Fermi's cautious words. In order to add to the fame of Fascist Italy, they boldly declared that an Italian scientist had become the first man in history to create a new element. People all over the world read the story and were amazed.

Fermi was angry. "I did not say I created a new element!" he told his friends. "A good scientist does not make such a claim when he cannot be sure of his facts." He sent his own story to the papers. It said he did not know whether he had created a new element or not.

But Fermi had little time for public arguments. He was planning new experiments. He wanted to make more careful studies of some of the elements that became radioactive when he bombarded them with neutrons. He wanted to know more about what happened when neutrons struck the cores of atoms of those elements.

One day he and his team were working with the element silver. Sometimes they created a lot of radioactivity in the silver, sometimes only a little.

"Why aren't the results always the same?" Fermi asked himself.

Then he wondered what would happen if the neutrons had to pass through another material before they struck the silver. He decided to find out.

He put some silver inside of a big block of paraffin. He put the neutron gun on the outside. The neutrons had to pass through the paraffin before they struck the silver.

Then he checked the silver with the Geiger counter.

Suddenly everyone in the room was shouting. The Geiger counter showed that the silver had become much more radioactive than ever before.

"It's absolutely fantastic! It's unbelievable!" they said.

Everyone looked at Fermi. "Why?" they asked.

Fermi could not answer them. He ate lunch alone that day. He wanted to think.

Carefully he went over in his mind some of the discoveries he had made. He knew, for example, that in his experiments an atom of silver became radioactive only if its inner core, or nucleus, was struck by a speeding neutron. Usually he had succeeded in making only a small number of silver atoms radioactive. This meant that only this small number had been struck at the core by neutrons.

But when Fermi had sent the neutrons through paraffin first, more of them had struck the targets he was hoping they would strike. Why had this happened?

Suddenly Fermi thought of an answer to his question.

"Paraffin contains a great deal of hydrogen," Fermi said to himself. "Neutrons passing through it must collide with the nuclei of many hydrogen atoms, and these collisions must slow the neutrons down before they reach the silver. Then these slowly traveling neutrons can find more targets as they pass through the silver than our neutrons did when they were traveling at greater speed."

He told the members of his team about his new theory.

"There is an easy way to prove whether it

is right or not," one of them said. "All we need do is use water in our experiment instead of paraffin. Water contains a lot of hydrogen too."

"Let's go!" someone shouted. "To the fishpond!"

They all ran to the fishpond in Professor Corbino's garden. They put their sample of silver under water at one end of the pond. They put the neutron "gun" under water at the other end. The neutrons would now have to travel the length of the pond under water before they could strike the silver.

They began the experiment. Fermi held the Geiger counter close to the silver. It clicked wildly.

"You're right!" someone shouted. "The water slows the neutrons down too!"

Fermi was grinning broadly. His theory had been proved.

As soon as reports of his work with radio-activity were printed, scientists everywhere wrote to congratulate him. He had made two important discoveries about the mysterious atom in less than one year.

He had proved that atoms of many substances could be made radioactive. He had discovered that slow neutrons can be better "bullets" than fast neutrons.

Fermi could not guess it at the time, but he was leading the whole world of science into what would come to be known as the Atomic Age.

7. A New Home

During the next few years Fermi received several invitations to teach at American universities.

"Shall we go?" he always asked Laura. "Shall we move to the United States?"

He was growing more and more worried about what was going on in Italy and the rest of Europe.

Mussolini had become the friend and ally of Adolf Hitler, the powerful new dictator of Germany. Hitler was threatening to seize some of Germany's neighbors by force. If Hitler started a war in Europe, it seemed very likely that Italy would be in it.

Laura still did not want to leave Italy. Like many others she did not believe that war would really come.

Then Mussolini said he was going to make some new laws. They would be like the new German laws against the Jews. Hitler hated Jews, and the laws he had made gave him the right to seize their property, throw them in jail, or kill them.

At first most Italians did not think Mussolini would really make such laws. "Our government is not always good," they said, "but it would never do anything as bad as that."

But Fermi was shocked and angry. Laura was a Jew. He didn't want his family to live in a country that passed laws against Jews. "Now we must leave Italy!" he said.

Laura too was indignant. "Now I am willing to go," she said. "But suppose Mussolini will not let you leave?"

They both knew that Mussolini would not want Italy's most famous physicist to leave the country.

"He will let me visit the United States, as I have done before," Fermi pointed out.

"You mean we should pretend to go to the United States on a visit, and then stay there?" Laura asked.

"Exactly," Fermi told her.

He wrote to Columbia University in New York to say he would be glad to teach in its physics department. He let the Italian newspapers report the news that he was going to America for six months.

Before Fermi and his family could leave, Mussolini did pass some laws against Jews. Fermi was more alarmed and angry than ever. Now he was afraid Laura might not be allowed to leave Italy.

Then he heard important news. He heard

that he might be given the Nobel Prize, the greatest honor a scientist could receive.

"If you win the prize, everything will be all right," one of his friends told him. "You will be invited to Sweden to accept it. Mussolini will be delighted. He will not even object if you announce that you are taking your family with you. Many Nobel prize winners take their families along to Sweden for the great prize-giving ceremony. From Sweden you can go to America."

"Yes," Fermi agreed. "Laura and the children will be safe—if I win the prize."

The days passed slowly. Finally, early one morning, the phone rang in the Fermi apartment.

"You will receive a call from Sweden this evening," a voice said. "Will you be at home?"

"Oh, yes!" Laura said, and ran to tell her husband. "Surely it must be the prize!" she said. "Why else would anyone be calling you from Sweden?"

That day seemed endless, but that evening the call from Sweden brought Fermi the news that he had been awarded the Nobel Prize for his brilliant work with neutrons. Minutes later the Fermi house was crowded with their friends. They brought food and wine. They said they wanted to celebrate the great news. They had really come to say good-bye. They knew they might never see the Fermis again once they left Italy.

On the day the Fermis took the train to Sweden, their friends gathered around them at the station.

"Suppose Laura is stopped from leaving at the last moment?" someone whispered. It was a thought in everyone's mind.

The Fermis climbed aboard the train with all the luggage they dared take with them.

Fermi accepts the Nobel Prize from the
King of Sweden for his work with neutrons.

They leaned out of the window to touch the hands of their friends once more. Fermi looked down the platform to make sure no policeman was coming.

"All aboard!" the conductor called at last. The train pulled out of the Rome station.

On December 10, 1938, Enrico Fermi received the Nobel Prize in physics from the hand of the King of Sweden. It was a great occasion.

For the Fermis an even greater occasion was their arrival in New York City less than a month later. They felt that they were about to start an entirely new life in the New World.

8. Chain Reaction

The Fermis were not yet settled in their new home when they had a visitor from Denmark. He was Niels Bohr, a famous physicist. He brought Fermi important news.

Bohr said that some German scientists, after reading of the work Fermi had done in Rome, had spent four years bombarding uranium with neutrons. These scientists had discovered that some uranium atoms split in two when neutrons struck them.

"And when the uranium atoms split," Bohr said, "they released energy! Do you realize where your work has led?" he asked Fermi. "Do you realize that this could mean a new source of energy for the world? Why, this could be as important as the discovery of electricity!"

"But electricity is useful only because a great deal of it can be created," Fermi said. "Will it ever be possible to release a really useful amount of energy from atoms? We must find out!" he decided.

He started immediately to organize a new team of workers. One member was a young

Danish physicist Niels Bohr

American. Another was a Canadian. A third was a Hungarian who had left his country because it too had laws against Jews.

"Creating a tiny amount of atomic energy is one thing," Fermi told his team. "To do that we would have to produce only a tiny stream of neutrons, and we know we can do that. But to get a lot of energy we would have to bombard uranium with a large and steady stream of neutrons. How can we obtain those neutrons?"

Fermi offered a possible answer to his own question.

"There is a theory," he said, "which would solve our problem if it could be proved to be correct. The theory is this: when a uranium atom splits and releases energy, it also releases some of its own neutrons. If that actually happens, some of the released neutrons might split more uranium atoms,

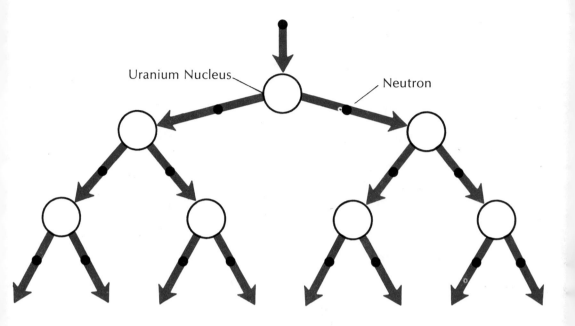

and this would release still more neutrons, and these neutrons would also split uranium atoms—and so on and so on.

"In other words," Fermi pointed out, "if we started by aiming a small stream of neutrons at some uranium, under certain conditions which we don't yet know, we might produce a 'chain reaction'—a chain of

75

atom splittings. Once we got it started, our uranium might go on bombarding itself with its own neutrons. And in that case the production of atomic energy might actually be possible."

To test this theory, Fermi knew it would be necessary to carry out many experiments.

Fermi believed that a chain reaction could be started only in a large "pile" of uranium. Only in a large pile, he thought, would the neutrons have a chance of hitting enough targets to start the chain. But just how large that pile should be was only one of the many problems that had to be solved.

He and his team worked for many months. During that time Adolf Hitler seized Czechoslovakia. No other country dared to try to stop him. Many people believed Hitler when he said his German army could defeat all the other armies of Europe.

The members of Fermi's team were deeply concerned about the future.

"German physicists know how to split uranium atoms too," they said. "If they learn to create a lot of atomic energy, they could use it to run ships. They might even use it to make powerful bombs. And Hitler might use those bombs to conquer the world! If it is possible to produce atomic energy, we must learn how to do it before the Germans do!"

Fermi did not want the German scientists to get ahead of him. "But," he said, "we can't go faster without more equipment and more scientists to help us. They both cost money. We do not have it."

Leo Szilard, the Hungarian, said, "We must write the President of the United States and ask him to give us the money we need."

"Do you think President Roosevelt would read a letter from men he never heard of?"

Fermi asked. "Of course not! Even if he read it, why should he believe what we say? Only a few people in the world have ever heard of atomic energy. Even we are not sure it can ever be produced in large quantities."

"He might not believe us," Szilard agreed. "But there is one scientist he would believe —Albert Einstein. I think we should ask Einstein for his help."

A few days later Szilard and two other scientists went to see Einstein. The great physicist listened to what they had to say. Then he agreed to sign a letter to President Franklin D. Roosevelt.

The letter began: "Some recent work by E. Fermi and L. Szilard ... leads me to expect that the element uranium may be turned into a new and important source of energy."

In the letter Einstein said he thought an atomic bomb might some day be made. He

Albert Einstein helped Fermi obtain government funds for his work.

also said that scientists in America should speed up their work with atoms and learn how to produce atomic energy before the Germans did.

The date on the letter was August 2, 1939. Less than a month later World War II started in Europe. France, England, and their allies were finally fighting the German army.

President Roosevelt believed the United States should be ready to defend itself. He decided that the government should help scientists like Fermi and his team.

Now Fermi had more money to spend. His team grew larger. He could afford to order more supplies—more uranium and more graphite, the slippery black stuff used in lead pencils. Fermi was using graphite, as he had once used paraffin and water, to slow up his speeding neutrons.

The uranium Fermi needed had to be pure, and little pure uranium was available. The graphite had to be pure too, and not much pure graphite was available, either.

"It will be months—maybe years—before we can get enough material to build a really big pile," Fermi said. "But as soon as we get enough for a small pile we will build that, and learn all we can from it."

The graphite came in blocks. Fermi and his team cut them into bricks and cut hollows for their uranium in some of the bricks. At the end of each work day their hands and clothes were black.

Laura Fermi wondered why her husband was always so dirty when he came home at night. Fermi could not tell her. By then he and his fellow scientists had been pledged to secrecy about their work on atoms.

The year 1941 was fast coming to an end. Hitler and his ally Mussolini, who had brought Italy into the war in June 1940, seemed to be winning the war in Europe.

Fermi had been working for almost two years on the problem of starting a chain reaction. By then other scientists in the United States were also working on some of the problems that would have to be solved if man was to produce atomic energy.

"I think it can be done," Fermi declared. "And some day, I hope, we shall do it. But we shall need tons of material—not the pounds of uranium and graphite we are using now. We shall have to build a pile bigger than this room!"

Then, on December 7, 1941, Japan attacked Pearl Harbor. Suddenly the United States was at war with Japan, and with Germany and Italy too.

American leaders said, "Now we must have atomic energy! We will bring together in one place all the scientists who have been working in this field and give them every possible assistance."

The place they chose was Chicago. Fermi moved there. Laura followed with the children as soon as the school year ended.

In Chicago Fermi was the leader of a new and bigger team. He set about building a new pile in a big room under the University of Chicago stadium. Nearby were rooms where the team could make the special equipment and instruments the work needed.

Slowly the big pile of graphite bricks began to grow. In it Fermi placed "control rods." They could prevent neutrons from reaching the uranium packed into the bricks. When these control rods were pulled out of the pile, neutrons could reach their targets.

Each day, as the pile grew, Fermi tested it and made calculations.

"We are coming closer to the right size," he said each day.

Then came the day when he said, "One more layer of bricks and I think our pile will be big enough to start a chain reaction."

The next morning, December 2, 1942, Fermi and all his assistants gathered in the big room under the stadium. Three men

stood on top of the huge pile. They had buckets of a special liquid that could stop the neutrons. Some scientists were afraid the pile might blow up or send out dangerous amounts of radioactivity, if a chain reaction started and could not be controlled.

Fermi was calm.

Inch by inch the last control rod was pulled out of the pile.

Geiger counters clicked faster and faster.

Suddenly Fermi smiled. "We have a chain reaction," he said.

He allowed the chain reaction to continue for 28 minutes. Then Fermi ordered his assistants to push the control rods back into the pile. The chain reaction ceased.

Fermi had proved that man could produce energy from splitting atoms, and that he could control the production of that energy.

The Atomic Age had begun.

9. Father of Atomic Power

The world's first atomic bomb was tested on the morning of July 16, 1945 in the middle of an empty desert in New Mexico.

It exploded with a flash as bright as the sun. A gigantic ball of fire rose into the sky. Smoke billowed out in the shape of a great mushroom. The earth shook. Deadly radioactive waves spread in all directions.

Enrico Fermi had helped make the bomb. For a year he and his family had lived at Los Alamos in New Mexico. Before the war Los Alamos had been a boys' school. The United States government had turned it into homes and laboratories for atomic scientists.

A tall fence surrounded the vast place. No one could enter or leave without a pass. Fermi had a bodyguard wherever he went.

The rest of the world did not even know that Los Alamos existed. Everything about it was kept secret. There Fermi and other scientists put to use their knowledge of atoms and how to split them. There they built the most powerful bomb man had ever made.

On August 6, three weeks after the test, an American plane dropped an atomic bomb on the Japanese city of Hiroshima. Three days later a second atomic bomb was dropped on the Japanese city of Nagasaki.

More than 100,000 people were killed by those two bombs. Thousands more, burned by radioactivity, were scarred for life.

Germany and Italy had already surrendered. On August 14 Japan surrendered too. World War II was over.

Many people said the United States had been wrong to drop atomic bombs on Japanese men, women, and children. Some of the scientists at Los Alamos were sorry that they had helped to build such a terrible weapon.

Enrico Fermi did not agree with them. "If we had not made atomic bombs," he said, "enemy scientists would have made them. It would have been worse for the world if someone like Hitler had used atomic bombs to win the war." But once the war was over Fermi did not want to work on weapons any longer.

"I don't like to work in secret," he said. "I believe that scientists should tell each other what they discover. And I want to teach young people in a university again. Training new scientists is one of our most important jobs."

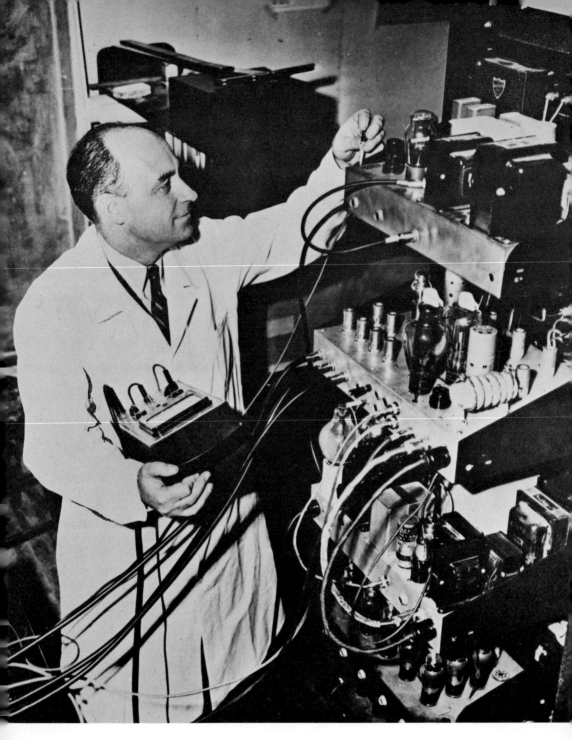
Fermi in his laboratory in Chicago.

Other Los Alamos scientists agreed with him. Some of them joined him at the University of Chicago, where the Institute of Nuclear Physics had been formed.

"We do not know nearly enough about the nucleus—the core—of the atom," Fermi said. "This must be the subject of our study."

At Chicago Fermi helped plan and build a new giant cyclotron, or atom smasher. It was finished in 1951.

Fermi took Laura to see it. "It makes atomic particles go around a circle at terrific speeds," he told her. "Then it shoots them out at targets. It will help us learn more about atoms."

He was especially proud of what his friends called Fermi's Trolley. It looked like a child's wagon, made of plastic. It ran around the rim of the big round cyclotron. The scientists used it to move equipment

Fermi's Trolley made atomic work safer.

while the cyclotron was working. They could control the trolley without getting close to the dangerous radiations from the atom smasher.

"I invented it," Fermi told Laura. "And I made every piece of it myself!"

In 1954 Fermi made a trip to Europe. He went as a citizen honored by his new homeland. A grateful American government had awarded him the Congressional Medal of

Merit. He had been named an advisor to the Atomic Energy Commission, a new government body set up to develop the uses of atomic energy.

Fermi was visiting Europe as a working scientist, not as a famous man. He wanted to talk to other physicists there about some of his new atomic theories. He wanted to talk to them about ways of using atomic energy in peace, not war. He was looking ahead to all the new work he planned to do.

He was tired when he left on the trip. He was very tired when he returned. Doctors examined him and discovered that he had cancer of the stomach. There was nothing they could do to help him.

A few weeks later, on November 29, 1954, Enrico Fermi died. He was 53 years old.

Scientists all over the world were stunned. Some used words to pay tribute to him.

Laura and Enrico Fermi at work shortly
before the noted scientist's death.

One American scientist said, "We won't see his like in a hundred years."

The members of the Atomic Energy Commission honored Fermi by giving his name to their annual award to an important scientist. Fermi himself had been the first winner of that award, now known as the Enrico Fermi Prize.

The University of Chicago gave his name to the Institute for Nuclear Physics. It is now called the Enrico Fermi Institute for Nuclear Studies.

And physicists — the men with whom Fermi had worked all his life — gave him the memorial he would probably have appreciated most of all. When a new element was created, bringing the number of known elements to one hundred, they named it fermium, in honor of the man they called the Father of Atomic Power.